AF342136

Mark Karlins

THE COURTYARD OF CONTINUOUS RETURNING

STATION HILL
TEXT
1981

Acknowledgements

Several of these poems have been published in *Origin* (Cid Corman), *Flute* (Brian McInerney), & *Lost Paper* (George Quasha).

I would particularly like to thank my wife emil for her hand in the crafting of this book. In our discussion of these poems, in their various stages of composition, her comments have helped lead the poems toward their final form. Her work is evident throughout.

This edition is published jointly by *Text Magazine* and Station Hill Press, and comprises a special issue *(#13)* of *Text,* which has been partially funded by a grant from the National Endowment for the Arts, a federal agency.

This book was typeset and produced at Open Studio in Rhinebeck, New York, a non-profit facility for writers and independent publishers, funded in part by grants from the New York State Council on the Arts and the National Endowment for the Arts.

Cover Design: Bruce McClelland
Cover Illustration: *Plan for a Monastery,* c. 820. Chapter Library, St. Gall (Switzerland)

ISBN 0-930794-46-x

Text Magazine, 298 St. Paul's Ave., Staten Island, NY 10304
Station Hill Press, Barrytown, New York 12507

for emil & Jacob Gareth

Preface

the animals
that move thru the scene

move thru the season—

a pool, the field,
three trees I sit by
in a shepherdly manner.

drowsiness stirs up,
refashions, the old stories,

receives in its realm
sleep's schemes & motherly odors.

they
      move   move again
shift   the language

my heart drives
drawing me deeper to find
herbs, grasses, cures
in the refuge of the forest.

it could have been any
one of us.
it wasn't, it was
her
who fell
falls still
when she leads us
that direction,
a dire straight way
into dark. nailed us
there. down. what she said
was. she said I am
a lonely house in a dark wood,
I am an old scholar bright in a dark house
at the edge of, at the end of, the world.
I read the page, I lift the form.

The Birth Poem

water broke our sleep.
to hear midnight draw from night's
two sides: judgment, mercy
sounding in the tautness of its line.
it is cold, but the stars pour
through our windows.

A Morning Tale

she said she dreamed a river

large swans
small whales
                under a bright blue sky
later black hours before evening

or before rain came
to the other side of the river.

for years it is morning
                & an appetite for everything.

———————————————————————————

the voice falters

an orange
falls
from the rowboat

& into the pond
        where her gaze goes
        & days deepen her eyes.

            on shore

swift runners.
they go where they say. no one returns.

———————————————————————————

in his boat
the lover advances backward,
casts a sheepish eye.

a steadiness
even when it is raining
& she is in a bad mood

                        the slow, slow
                        strokes
                            of the oars.

one returns.
& it is spring
                & the heat of the body.

____

as for what the eye sees
                        it is winter.
blood remembers summer
                    & promise,
a body a dry light flies out of.

her father is the ape-faced man
coming out of the wood
                        toward her,
wanting to make peace.
snow fills the imprint
of his shoes
    even before he is gone & after,
    the erased evidence of the errand.

snow is warm
to her foot.
a bell rings
        deep
        in the bottom
        of the pond.

The Room

the wine
flowery & strong.
deep purple plums,
apples, cakes.
certain signs
& promises
forgetfulness
hasn't quite
swallowed up,
but when I enter
I go forward,
I go back;

there is no place.

Snow White

to live always with children
is to be haltered at unity,
door that opens inward

rose-trellised dusk-cottage
to play deftly at house,
be mother to small men

rose soft mouth
door for outward, apple
thru which the world enters

The Courtyard of Continuous Returning

grey stone rigid, dusk's air shifts
a wall,
how or why

it drew me
the next day

the day after that,
still does, flirts

delivers images desire forms
fastening so much
at one place, time

I want to push back
entering make a door
to go thru

to be in service
of continuous summoning,
an impossible blue
light on the foliage

bright moon
in the little marble pool
a woman beside,
her hand stirring soft thru the water

until synapse
grace
for all my respectful delay
leaves us no longer separate

yet it is to walk inside
with an outsider's yearning,
mind of the shtetl
stubbornly resisting apparent calm

inside with roses, sycamore, ailanthus
answering what awed me awake

as if that could satisfy

there is a deepened brightness
in her eyes

flames that tangle me,
love's light entwining

tradition tells of, marks
in clear strong lines

this feeling I have everytime
I am not taken in
by the daily little things

helps assure our own continuance,
channeling

all,
a river
that rush
between narrow banks

love's limits
a light how many ways I approach

leads toward an image
solid, almost enough
to say what she is
or can be

to set some boundary
say a piled stone wall
around

a pool

emerging somehow
in open sea

but that's not it
never could be

if spoken

my own breath
dispersing

the real
image behind the image

leading me out

I walk thru the house
hitting edges,
                    a chaos
seeking
bounds.

lost,
        you are
        a root
        growing
        in hell,

tho
your face
draws me on.

Junkyard

moon
falling
into
rust

an odor—
damp air and ruin

red iron
bound
in a circle
of pines

draws what light
that sphere sustains

and beyond
the trees
the hills
as plain,

the form
as fiercely
tranquil

and beyond that

the dead,

the body turning

a night into thought.

Hear
what he loved:
Eldorados, Impalas,
doing sixty
beneath cedars
on an old dirt road.

He had their speed.
It sufficed.

hands curled tight
on the wheel
for curves

to ride
so that all things
are past

in the rearview mirror
branches
stars

beyond that

nothing

gas pedal.
foot
drawn down
by love,
the fear
of it

moving
deep
into
what
was
real,

the road's curve
driving winter
    thru his skull.

red stain
of the moon
in his flesh

glass
piled
deep
on
earth

moon
falling
into
rust

after illness

sipping
jasmine
the small
white flowers
now swelled
now limp

          her face,
          the skin itself
          brighter.

the steamy panes.
the dark
red
chrysanthemums.

A Dance in Two Days

1.

eyes ache again ungainly
night my window willows
the roof so quiet until

how long we linger, however well.

2.

reform this form. shape again.
gain is the said. she is
so,
        in the manner
                        of a dance.

her foot

        to earth.

3.

upon this pivot place
is us. walking is always
out into. thrust of the night

bright air.

4.

wake me well from my languaging
slumber. hot sun on the beach
bakes my such & such knowledge.
the sweet bright
oil has its light.   undoubt me.

Okakura and the Art of Flower Arrangement

[The Birth of Flower Arrangement]

after rain
flowers.

those scattered
set

in rough
clay vessels.

a trace of,
the way your hand moves

[*Sleep*]

Chou Mou Shu's
prized attendant
washes leaves
with the rabbit-hair brush
and Chou Mou Shu
sleeps in a boat
that his dreams
may drink from the lotus.

[*Gravity*]

the exchange
articulates
wherever it is
he moves—
solicitude.
earth lifts
as his foot,
content in this
energy, falls
& draws
his days
within love's orbit,
its course particular
to seasons.
cold water
carried back
from the mountain spring
to water the winter plum.

if I think / & image this thinking
as her / as harped

as the river dawn's
lower regions
where streams still flow
geared to the rotation

the Hudson widens,
quiets.
flat deepest blue
drifts, leaves
low tide mud.
clatter of starlings
toward Crueger's

island
we also went toward.
                a path
of tight, hard earth
to a level of smallest
white flowers. summer's
dark grass stiffly over

where we stopped
(before Crueger's)
before anything less
than these flowers
she carried me toward
& lowered her body against

& now Manhattan
& memory : the woods

a garden
ten years in keep
to tend, that those flowers
could her restore.

Night, a Boundary

1.

toss under goose-feathers.
wind
down the chimney.
a bird's long note
bids an old dream
          thrust thru inland fog.

2.

stirred,
the stench up from the bog
gets into everything.
a trace of rot,
an outside
taken in,
given
back
divided
by 1.

a large grey dog

        along the edge.

James F. Cooper

immersed
to rise anew
beyond
this fragment—
'there is no such thing
on earth'
the upward
turning, o
the heart
does take the world
each point
dawn
the preparation
on a boat that glides
to the bank of a lake
to come to terms
plunges
into the
opening

between
pines
up
from
the
bank
into the calm
of his own
birth

. . . .

can a man go further, if not
what then? nothing beyond it?
a darkness
(   )
in the aging
of a man
thrown back
upon himself
who becomes
contained
in the neutrality
of his own
universe
the slowly
changing
contours
foreshadowed
in the doubleness
of his tensions
escape & return

the birches
are frail
so much so they're barely
image
along the stared at
lake side
on to which his mind projects
a city
the concentric
steps
taken
around the heart
amidst
the solemn

pageant
of a willful people
rejoicing

all souls
later
to rise

no such thing on earth,
or in heaven?

but the birds had swift steps
on the new
grass
beside him.

———————————————————————————————

the imprecisions

of a half-closed planet

pulled
to a fate
the sentence might take
if allowed
an actual land

the beginning
first half-formed words
envision

night at its resolve
into the soft body
of the dark trees climbing
below the slate of the river gorge

unbinding all into fable,
that total

possibility in the presence
of an unknown   :

temple

dark
woods

heart

Milkweed Pod

her touch.
seeds spill

wind

fills
the land.

Night, a Boundary

went out into the middle,
pattern
we enter
& entering
keep *them*
at bay,
I mean
touch me.
bright sky,
moon,
broken stone
at its apex an angle
of what *we* tongue
yet still outside us
impenetrable as a cat's eye.
the branches, where they allow
it all filters down so simply;
light
thru which the world
carries in.
dark's an old story,
a hag's,
hedge rider,
slight boundary
defends us from.
it gets into our ears.

but I want to hear it literal,
wind thrusting thru a network of branches
& ending there,

outside us.

The Suitors Approach
the Glass Mountain

light under the eyelids   .   mountain
is the utterance of the mind
of the king

the procession
of solitary
walkers

warmed by the radiance of glass

.   .   .   .   .

devouring, graceful earth
mouth to the self's migration

                    earth issues prior to man

the fatherhood   /   dreamer

the disk of the moon floats alone in the sky

Imago Mundi

cast into the thick
dust at the foot of
his bed,
>   an image
>   of the world

evokes a time
to hear him in
or air the causes
that led him there,
sick, bleary-eyed,
& feverish till
[bright floor
dotted with oceans,
forests,
everests the size
of a thumbnail]
the sun rose
pink hot light
on a still damp moon.
there is a sickness
can be cured,
going back
is entrance,
an eternal
return.
Bruce talks wolves
tracks in snow
now melting
into spring
autumn by the
smell of the burnt
leaves

by the roadside
thyme the summer
the heat of
coming up under winter's
first soft snow.
confusion seasons
the obvious woods
an oak today
the lumberman splits
for the tale-side
hearth, thus its
growth is a going,
its fall
a fire,
the light that fed it.
Jack autumns too,
awoke in his own bed
discovering as the day
became as dim
as his eyes had become
he had forgotten,
thinking he'd reached
his heart through
the giant's harp,
who he was.
economics. drove him,
is an inflated
relation.
red berries become
a pot of gold,
his heart
is art is up
for grabs;
it is to be clever
& not to hear.

rain did beat
on the cottage
window as he
woke, falling
out of his own
song into something
which wasn't spring
at all.
never would be.
Jack autumns.
yet the trees were
red &
yellow, bird
colors as bird song
is talk
gets the rain
the day
in its specific
as sun does show
suddenly how our
weathers change.
seasons do [as
a language does,
addressed to
old grizzly beard's
own soft womanly heart
to hear]
& aren't
confusion.

        it was all about
        forgetting

           stones talk

as do
roses

          waking
          her

in her lover's house

Daylight Is Its Own Limit

as water does
or blood or the odor of
the dog coming in
from the rain
makes the room
too tangible for any of us,
there is a speech
that insists its
intricate

direction
keeps us
many ways at once.
we are plural & interrupted.
incurable,
Plato said,
meaning the souls in Hades
are dark enough
to see when a shadow
has substance. which is what
I want to take into morning
& not have the light understand.

a measure

how the flower
burns

& all night
the tree out back

controls the way
I am about to enter

The text face for this edition is Kennerley, with Palatino titles. The edition consists of seven hundred and fifty copies, of which forty-three have been signed and numbered.